THIS NOTEBOOK BELONGS TO ....

CONTACT ....

See our range of fine, illustrated books, ebooks, notebooks and art calendars:
www.flametreepublishing.com

This is a **FLAME TREE NOTEBOOK**
Published and © copyright 2017 Flame Tree Publishing Ltd

FTNB 155 • 978-1-78664-620-0

Cover image based on a detail from
Pink Flamingoes by Gerritt Vandersyde (1898–1970)
© Look and Learn/Bridgeman Images

Born in Camberwell in London, Gerritt Vandersyde is best known for his illustrations for advertising, books and magazines, with one of his prints being used in the background of Stanley Kubrik's *A Clockwork Orange*. This image portraying a flock of flamingoes residing next to a lake was originally used in the magazine *Once Upon a Time*.

FLAME TREE PUBLISHING | The Art of Fine Gifts
6 Melbray Mews, London SW6 3NS, United Kingdom

All rights reserved. Printed in China. Created in the UK.